"Consider the lilies of the field,

how they grow; they toil not,

neither do they spin:

And yet I say unto you,

that even Solomon in all his glory

was not arrayed like one of these."

Matthew 6: 28-29

Consider the Lilies

Poems by Diana Prince, PhD.

AuthorHouse™
1663 Liberty Drive
Bloomington, IN 47403
www.authorhouse.com
Phone: 1-800-839-8640

Published by AuthorHouse 09/09/2015

ISBN: 978-1-4670-3137-0 (sc)
ISBN: 978-1-5049-3444-2 (hc)

Library of Congress Control Number: 2011917207

Print information available on the last page.

Any people depicted in stock imagery provided by Thinkstock are models,
and such images are being used for illustrative purposes only.
Certain stock imagery © Thinkstock.

This book is printed on acid-free paper.

authorHOUSE®

Contents

Consider The Lilies

There is a shelter on this plain.
The world itself embraces you.
And God who gave us caverns, caves
And trees in shade to rest—

Gave birds to race in clouds,
Spiders to spin bright nets,
And trees reaching into sunlight—
      All to delight us.

All the world reaching skyward.

The birds poised on that air
Do not worry that the blue glass of the sky
Will shatter and leave them
Windless and broken,

Knowing they are meant to fly
And earth, itself, will never be enough.

Rest in His arms
When all this world comes rushing past,
Tumbling like birds
Through winds of wings and sound
With God, Himself, to hold you fast.

In His Own Image

He knows the number
of incomparable stars
that go on forever—

He is their fire.

He is the pulse of galaxies
like angel choirs.

Einstein and Galileo
could not breach
that place outside of time
and out of reach—

That symmetry of stars
In Heaven's floor,

And man—
With God's breath filling every pore.

This is the gift to man he sent—

That we are dust
But dust
        Magnificent.

What If God Spoke?

I wondered what if
God came and said,
"I love you" to the world—

In His proper, serious voice,
And we saw Him standing there
probably in white.

Not a dream—
but real.

It would prove everything.
It would be on the evening news.

Otherwise,
how would we ever know for sure
we were not just
a distant experiment
Spinning untended in a galaxy.

Meanwhile,
      I watched the birds
      trace circles in the sky,
      And saw a bee
      inside a rose,
      While sun-filled clouds
      pressed near,
      And morning glories
      trembled in the wind.

In that sweet summer day I heard
The way he says, "I love you" without words.

This Side Of Heaven

The architecture of the heart
is simple, plain
And irrefutable.

Clinging to the rooms of the heart,
Dreams, sighs, regrets
Unfold like pages endlessly.

And in the worn parts
        of the heart
Where our oldest memories live,
They scatter like glass
To live and live again.

They will not be silent.

They are like the blue fire
of the morning glories

Leaping up from summer grass.

Genesis

Sun light into forests pouring,
the bright wings of eagles soaring.

This is my ocean,
Mountain, star and sky.

Of all somewheres we wandered to,
of all the times
      we danced around
      this point of time,

It brings us here to where it all began.

Snowflakes come swirling
      from an endless sky,

And we are dancing on the light.

Raindrop

Light trembles
and hangs
interminably
in a drop of rain—

Ready to fall
from a leaf.

God's own hand
traces the physics of light
swimming in water.

Light caught
inside a raindrop—

A silent, perfect world.

Finding God

What we love becomes our treasure
and defines us
Like a moth to flame.

We are pulled endlessly
to everything that glitters
and is gone.

How do we plant our roots in solid ground?
And where do we begin?
We are restless like a child's kite
tugging in the wind.

We wait for someone
to reveal it all.
We drift like reddened leaves
And then we fall.

Waves leap for us
only to pull us back.

We often lose our way,
and home is out of reach.
Even the ocean claims
our footprints on the beach.

We can feel pity
and we can feel rage,
But even history leaves us—
        Turns its page.

Days crumble into time
and then are gone
After the dazzling earth
puts on her show.

When we have tired finally,
of all the things
That pull us in their flow—

Chase God.
Chase God, relentlessly

And never let Him go.

Mary And The Angel Gabriel

The whole world hushed
Waiting for Mary's answer,
Beneath the wings
That spread invisibly—

Like light that dashes
from the sun
in early dawn,
And catches like a fire in every tree.

Birds fell in flight
to waiting trees
where every leaf was blessed.

Even the tired earth pressed near
to hear her soft voice utter "Yes".

Then with a tremulous surprise
with that small sound that echoed her consent,

There came alive the blazing fire
of God's own Son,
for which this world was meant.

Tangible Prayer

In the aftermath
      Of a prayer
            Just-sent-to-God—

Silence and rose petals.

Jesus In The Rose Garden

He sat upon her lap,
her little son
who lightly opened petals one by one,
and let them fall upon the ground.

They swirled and fell,
in pieces to the ground,
and glittered in the light
without a sound.

And in that sparkling, whirling race,
It brought a smile to the little face.

"Again," He laughed,
"Again!"
Watching the blossoms
fall in sweet repose.

"Again," he laughed, "Again!
and mother, please,
Tell me, again, the story of the rose."

Madonna

Tiny curled fingers
fumble now with Mary's curls.
And little hands hold tightly
to the scattering of hair
That falls around him
like a veil there.

Her mouth speaks softly,
      syllables of air.

"Ýou are my song, my little one.
You are the words
That leave my heart undone."

Creation

We inhale
> The pure science of
> cold and remarkable stars.

The premise is this—
> we walk through this garden,
And become inflamed
by one bright butterfly.

The orchids are radiant,
The sun is solid like gold
> and moves imperceptibly.

God is like that.

Particles of small worlds
bourne on light
> are crystallized.
> Immaculate.

Every moment counts.

The world rests
> In the funnel of that heat.
> Life, persistent

Irrepressible.

God And The Bee

God is the buzzing
of the tiger-colored bee

And the fierce thrashing
of transparent wings.

And when he slumbers
in the perfect rose,
He is at perfect peace.

And I suppose
      God is the honey
        sweet like liquid gold—

The unbearable sweetness
only God can bring.

He is
      the everything of everything.

Song Of The Earth

Your handiwork
Awakes in silence.

The sun coming up;
the glory of the farm,
the chicken coops,
the staring cows,
Gray geese.

Running like clockwork,
clicking and clicking
Like the noise of a tongue
clicking the roof of the mouth.

Smell the fern
And the rich field smell
of buttercups.

Father, the stars rain down
and I am gleaming.
Washed clean,
I am gleaming like a rock.

God, big as a mountain,
Scoop me up.
In one long sleeve,
raise me above the corner
of the world
Where I can look down
          on this land and sea

And sing out
from the deep nest of Your hand.

Small Kindnesses

He wanted to do
Big things for God—
Preaching oceans away
or writing a perfect play
that touched man's soul.

And now it was too late—
So he continued on
in his three-bedroom
on a cul-de-sac.
Day after day
in ordinary ways.

And then one week,

>At lunchtime he held the door
>for the fragile lady with a cane.
>
>He helped a stranger
>change a tire in the rain,
>While rain ran down his neck
>and soaked his head,
>and other passing cars
>drove by instead.
>
>When his wife burned
>the cake she tried to make,
>He said, "We'll add more frosting
>   on the cake."
>
>When his son lost the ball game
>at the field that day
>and tears rolled down his cheek,
>Dad stopped for pizza, and he said,
>   "There will be many other games to play."

Somewhere God smiled among the angel wings
Because he sees the very smallest things.

The Pulse Of Life

God is not the sun
even when He moves
inside the sun,
And rests His feet in stars.

This is His perfect secret—
  He is in all things,
  but He is not those things.

He is the thread
that binds and breathes—

All that He is
Lasts always and remains

simple and incorruptible,

This endless God
Who will not be contained.

Angels Walking

The angels walk among the stars.
Their gowns, blown skyward
by the dust of clouds,
Sail out behind them cold and clean.

There are a thousand things
That move unseen.

And angels we mistake for dreams or clouds
Trail in the pure wind like a kite.
The branches swirl under their feet—
A sea of rooftops
and the city lights.

There are so many things
we leave unsaid.

There are so many angels out tonight.

This Thing Called Life

The taste of April
is full of wild violets
and windy days.

Shirts fluttering from clotheslines
Like paper Chinese kites,
Tugging to be free;
And the flowers, too, must
Pull against their roots.

Trying to climb towards light and God,
They push against the rich, blue air.

The Magdalene

You would have saved him
but his fate was cast,
And hungry hearts
          were waiting for the flame
That blazed and died
upon a cross that day.

But still remains that moment sweet—
The fall of golden hair
          upon his feet,
The color of burnt leaves.

Swimming in tears,
you saw the crowd dissolve.
Just you and he were there.
He touched your head
with words that reassured,
"Forgiven" was the only word you heard.

You understood it all—
the gentle Soul he was,

          The man, the God,
          The agony, the love.

What You Do In My Name

The man at the shelter was wounded,
But his loss was not one eyes could see.
I felt what he felt in that instant.
For a moment, I thought he was me.

The man at the shelter was weary
And life was too much to resist—
But one mother held him, a lifetime ago,
And still he remembers her kiss.

The man at the shelter had passed us—
A child in playgrounds and halls,
Brushed shoulders with us on bright city streets—
Behind his invisible walls.

The man at the shelter was at once
both a child and a man. It was odd—
I knew in his eyes and his hunger
The man at the shelter was God.

Jesus Poem

This is the Jesus
Who walks in flowers.
       There is no gray anywhere.
The air is silk.

He strides on flowers
like rain
       that falls and bends and nourishes
       but does not break.

Each flower is a galaxy
       of leaves and stems—

       All these worlds under Him.

And even me.
He reaches in
Catching my heart
in one hand.

The way you hold
a small bird—
a warm small life
beating and beating.

What August Tells Us

In August, before the melancholy
strains of fall
Hover like ghosts
in leaves,

There is a peculiar clarity.

Like a photo lens
focused in sharp relief,
Before the blurring
of time and the senses.

We know then
that there is more to life
than these voices,
this clutter, this noise.

Birds sing among the rooftops,

      And angels walk in sunlight.

The Resting Place

Back when the world was innocent,
And angels to that dark world bent
To fill it with a blazing light—
They brought Him forth that holy night.

And in the room they kept the sheep,
They built for him a place to sleep,
With wood the color of dark wine
Fresh cut and smelling still of pine.

The years moved on to other days.
It seemed the world became a maze
Of breaking hearts and storms above—
All needing to be fixed with love.

And so he journeyed thirty years,
And with his words, he touched their tears.
Each breaking heart he sought to save
Could not forget his eyes, his gaze.

Until that day upon the hill
Men staked on following their will—
And underneath a darkening sky,
Put Kindness on a cross to die.

To make the cross, the soldiers found
Wood pieces scattered on the ground.
Some plain and simple cuts of pine
Still marked with lines and black with time.

And on that cross, He laid his head—
The same wood from that Baby's bed.

New Life

This is not a shadow life
That lingers in a fog or dream,
No pale half-life
        drifting endlessly.

We are the shadows
Resurrected.

It is life with bite.
The vinegar smell of earth—
Clouds stained the
        color of roses.

The methodical ocean crush on sand
That repeats and repeats
        and repeats.

There is a thread sewn
        noiselessly
        through every hour.

God is calling us home,
        One by one.

Angels

Angels are comet-white,
Flashes out of God's
       correct and bluest sky.

They find us. And wake us.
And shake us. And shape us.

Angels reaching in.
White fingers opening the blossom
of the heart.

Letter To God

I remember her in mornings
And how she used to run
Along the shore with me to find
Bright seashells in the sun.

She knew the words to every poem—
And we could talk for hours.
And when the morning glories came
We walked through endless flowers.

She knew the sweet old Irish songs
And sang them sweet and low,
But that was long before I knew
Mothers could really go.

She left me seven years ago—
It seems like yesterday.
And no one since has sung her songs,
And yet her music stays.

Even today in winter's cold
I'm sure that she must be
So near you in your brightest cloud,
Give her a hug from me.

To God In Winter

In spring I never heard you there
Behind me on the wooden stair,
And yet somehow you steered my way
Through roads where apple blossoms lay.

In summer, unexpectedly
I'd find you in a leaf or tree—
Or on the greenest hillside where
Wind passed like fingers through my hair.

And now in Autumn's golden light,
I know you linger out of sight.
I walk through reddened leaves in fall
And know you never left at all.

When birch trees lean into the wind
And then the snowy fields begin,
The cardinal spreads its scarlet wing
And icy winter branches cling.

Walk with me then against the tide.
Stay every moment at my side.
So cold and barren trees may bring
Your certain promise of the spring.

About the Author

Diana Prince has a Master's Degree in English and a Master's Degree in Philosophy from California State University at San Diego. She completed a doctorate in Psychology at United States International University.

Dr. Prince has published in several poetry magazines including *Roanoke Review*, *Southern Poetry Review*, and *Western Review*. She published *Blackbird Spring*, a book of her poetry, and edited *Woman Soul*, a collection of work by women poets. She collaborated with two other poets to write *The Bedtime Book*, a volume of children's poetry.

She has worked as an Aerospace technical writer, and as a college professor in the English and Philosophy departments at National University.